*Sandy
Fox*

*Phil.
4:6-7, 13*

LORD RENEW MY HOPE

BY

SANDRA FOX

xulon PRESS

Contents

Acknowledgments

My sincere thanks to my husband, Will, for all his continuous support and encouragement. I could not have done this without you.

Thanks to Rev. Constance Frey and Rev. Rosemarie Brown for their special help in proof-reading and recommendations.

Thanks to my daughter, Betsy, for being an example of living and loving with hope.

Forward

Although the Bible predicts there will be difficult times during the "last days," it seems we
are never ready when they actually come our way.
We have all heard, "It is not what happens to you but
how you respond that is important." However, even
the strongest Christian can be negatively impacted
when the "storms of life" grow to such an intensity
that the Bible is hard to understand, God feels too far
away, and the comfort of friends is not sufficient to
stem the erosion of our faith.

That is exactly where our family found ourselves
when we experienced the "long goodbye," Nancy
Reagan's description of her experience with her
husband's battle with Alzheimer's. When my dad
was diagnosed with the same debilitating disease, we
had no idea how stressful the process or how much
our faith would be tested. It was during that experience that I began to see the correlation – but also the
distinct differences – between faith and hope. Painful
experiences may not completely wreck our faith but
can play havoc with our hope.

This book is a "must-read" for anyone who needs their hope restored.

Rev. Alton Garrison
Assistant General Superintendent of the Assemblies
   of God

Introduction

When I tell women that I'm writing a book on hope, there is usually a cry in their heart to hear more. This book was written for them – for every woman going through a difficult time, struggling to hang onto the promise God has given them. Every woman whose heart has cried out, "Lord, renew my hope".

Peace – We all want peace in our lives, peace in our families, peace in the world. But many times all we see is bickering, lies, fighting, and wars. Our jobs can be in question. Prices continue to rise. Our health may decline. Where is peace?

That flame seems to flicker and die.

Love – We are told that the greatest if these is love. But what we experience is misunderstandings and unforgiveness. Estrangements and divorce are rampant. People spend time gossiping or not speaking to each other. Families and marriages crumble. Where is the love? That flame also flickers and may go out.

Faith – The Word says that "without faith it is impossible to please God." We live in a society that says everyone does what is right in their own eyes. We are told it doesn't matter what you believe; just be good. All roads lead to heaven. We are weighted down with disappointments and discouragement. Where is faith when you feel like giving up? The flame begins to flicker.

Hope – But many have not lost their faith – they have lost their hope. Lord, renew my hope that I may ignite peace, love, and faith. Show me who to hope in and what to hope for.

There are over 130 verses with the word hope in the Bible. According to the dictionary, hope means to be confident.... to trust.....to expect....to look forward to. Hope is knowing the truth and acting on it.

Wait and HOPE for and expect the Lord;
Be brave and of good courage
And let your heart be stout and enduring.
Yes, wait for and HOPE for and expect the Lord.

Psalm 27:14 (AMP)

Chapter 1

Hope Again

*God wanted to make the unchanging nature of His
purpose very clear to the heirs
of what was promised, He confirmed it with an
oath. God did this so that, by two unchangeable
things in which it is impossible for God to lie,
we who have fled to take hold of the HOPE
offered to us may be greatly encouraged.*

Hebrews 6:17-18 (NIV)

S ea captains use latitude and longitude to plot their courses. Even in storms when they cannot see, their instruments tell them where they are going.

The writer of Hebrews tells us we have two fixed points. We have a latitude and a longitude also, His character and His word. If you feel lost in the storm of life and circumstances – there is a glimmer of hope…. a way to find your way home.

These two fixed points of latitude and longitude never change so we can know where He is. We can look at any circumstance and find God. He has given us His coordinates.1

His character is our latitude.

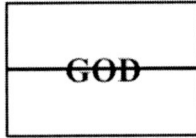

He is good.(Psa.34:8), He never changes. (Heb.13:8) He is fixed and true. (Psa. 19:9) He will not lie or go back on His word. (Heb. 13:8)

He is just and loving. (Gal. 2:20 and Jn. 3:16) His character is definite - we can count on Him.

The other fixed point is longitude—His word.

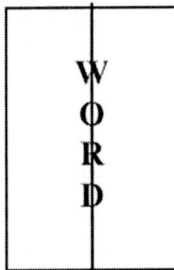

In the beginning was the Word and the Word was with God, and the Word was God." (Jn.1:1) He spoke His word into being and made provision for our sins and forgiveness. In Genesis, "God said...." for each creation. His word is strong and powerful. We have His word and God cannot lie.

By these two fixed points, our latitude and longitude- we can always find God.

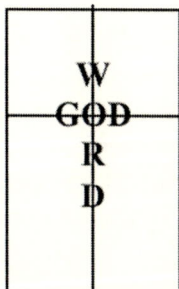

Ever found yourself saying – "did God really say that? Did He really mean that?" In Genesis 3:1, the serpent said, Did God really say that....? Jesus confronted the devil by saying, "It is written". (Matt. 4:4) And in Hebrews 6, the word says that it is impossible for God to lie.

A family story of hope was told by Alton Garrison in Today's Pentecostal Evangel. His father, a preacher and teacher was stricken with Alzheimer's. His mother, a godly pastor's wife and prayer warrior, was the caregiver. She became physically and emotionally exhausted. When she became "down" - discouraged – she began to wonder, where is God when you need Him most?

Alton began to pray and tell God that when his Dad passed-he would be in God's presence. But what if something were to happen to his mother. She has lost her faith. The Holy Spirit showed him the truth. She had not lost her faith, she had lost her hope.2

Many in the body of Christ are in this position today. They have become discouraged and depleted. Where is God when you need Him? They need more than trite phrases like – get a grip – or the glass is half full. There are many wounded warriors. Satan wants to discourage you. He can manipulate circumstances but he cannot change God's word.

Have you lost faith? NO - but you may have lost hope! There are many sermons on love and faith but few on hope. Faith is education—faith comes by hearing the word. Hope is emotion. Hope is morale.

We need our hope resurrected. We need to expect, to dream, to desire, to anticipate. If faith is dynamite—then hope is the fuse. The attack is against our hope. If Satan cannot defeat you scripturally, he will try to defeat you mentally and emotionally.

For whatever was written in earlier times was written for our instruction, that through perseverance and the encouragement of the Scriptures- we might have HOPE.

Romans 15:4 (ASV)

We try to look forward and figure things out, but we can not see ahead. So we get scared, unsure, feel lost, feel like there is no rescue in sight. The best way to handle the "jitters"???? Don't try to see the future – look to the past. Look at all the times that God has been there. In the Old Testament God was constantly calling His people to remember.

So remember what He has done for you in the past.

- at a wall of water in front of you?
- with an army coming up behind you?
- When you were in the wilderness with nothing to eat – who fed you?
- Where has God met you before and always shown Himself faithful?
- How many times did the money come, help arrive, or comfort appear – when you needed it most?

Do not try to muster up hope for what is ahead. Look back and be assured and acknowledge His faithfulness in the past. Psalm 143 says, In your faithfulness answer me, O Lord.

Abraham...who contrary to HOPE, in HOPE believed...according to what was spoken.

Romans 4:18 (NKJ)

Abraham in hope believed what God had said to him, even though there were circumstances working against his hope.

-destroyers of hope-

There are three things that can destroy our hope.

1. <u>Stop reacting to what you see.</u> Abraham didn't weaken at the circumstances. Faith does not deny reality—circumstances are real. Relationships can be bad. Your health can be declining and your checkbook can be lacking.

   We need to focus on the grapes (God's promises) – not on the giants (problems). As the spies came back from the promised land, ten spies concentrated on the giants in the land. However, Caleb and Joshua chose to focus on the grapes that were in the land. They saw the good land that the Lord was about to give them.

2. Another hope destroyer is when <u>we begin to question God's word -</u> the promises. Satan loves to whisper in our ear – did God really mean that? Abraham did not question God or say that he did not understand enough.

3. Another hope destroyer - <u>when you think it is up to you to fulfill a promise.</u> Remember Sarah and Ishmael! It has been said that we are microwave Christians. We want answers right away, but we have a crock pot God. The word tells us to wait and tarry.

May the God of HOPE fill you with all joy and peace in believing, that you may abound in HOPE by the power of the Holy Spirit.
Romans 15:13 (NKJ)

(The amplified says to be overflowing with hope.)

Now, how do we develop hope? God is the source of hope and hope is supplied by the Holy Spirit. When the Israelites crossed through the Red Sea – there were 2 ½ million people. Not just one hundred or two hundred people. And there were animals and wagons too. God thinks big!!

Imagine providing manna for that many people – every day. Fifteen tons of manna a day were required. And they also needed water- that would be about eleven million gallons of water. Our God is big!!

So it is not hopeless. What do you need hope for in your life? Take time to write on paper your hope promise. Habakkuk 2 says to write the vision and make it plain. Sometimes we need to be reminded of what God has said. Hold your hope-promise up to the Father. God is bound by His word.

Questions for Discussion or Reflection

1. Write out your hope promise.
   (Habakkuk 2:2 says to write the vision and make it plain.)

2. Think of some hope builder songs to sing this week.
   i.e.- God Will Make a Way & Nothing is too Difficult for Thee

3. Meditate on Psalm 56.

Chapter 2

Hope – God Sees

We have this HOPE as an anchor for the soul, firm and secure.

Hebrews 6:19 (NIV)

What do you do when life has dealt you a hard blow?

- Your husband served you with divorce papers
- The bank is to foreclose on your mortgage
- You have to file for bankruptcy
- Your child is suspended from school
- You need to sign him into rehab
- Doctor's report says it's terminal -or chronic—you have to live with it

You feel like you are groping through a tunnel. You feel depressed, disillusioned, frustrated, embarrassed, bitter, angry. You are beginning to lose hope that anything will ever change. And you wonder— does God know where I am?

-anchored in Christ-

In John 16 we read that in the world we will have tribulations, trials, distress, frustrations—but we're to be of good cheer, confident, certain—that He Has overcome the world and has conquered it for us. So the question is not whether you will have a storm in your life – but the question is – how will you handle it? What will you draw on to get your strength and encouragement?

The Amplified version states in Hebrews 6:19, that this anchor of the soul cannot slip and cannot breakdown under whoever steps out upon it – a hope.

Sometimes knots can be a nuisance - knots in the fine chain of a necklace, knots in your shoelaces. Bows are so much prettier but they're not strong enough to hold a hard connection.1 Before you tie a knot you want to make sure that what you are tying it to—can hold! The best looking knot in the world will do you no good if it is tied to a life jacket, a buoy, a person, a church. We must tie our knot to the solid anchor of Jesus Christ.

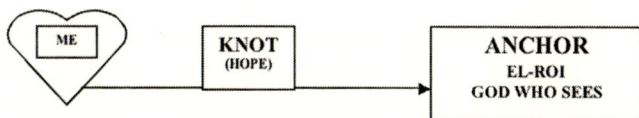

Why are you downcast O my soul? Why so disturbed within me?
Put your HOPE in God,
for I will praise Him, my Savior and my God.

Psalm 42:5 (NIV)

Do you you think that God doesn't know what you're going through? Do you feel forgotten? Do you feel insignificant?

-Hagar needed hope-

Hagar, an Egyptian slave, encountered God in the desert and addressed Him as El Roi - -the God who sees me. She was thrown out like a dirty rag, used and cast aside. She bundled up her few possessions and headed out the door. Where is her hope? Where is God? Does He see what is happening to her?

It was the custom in Mesopotamia in that day – the Code of Hammurabi - for a barren wife to have her handmaid bear her children. Such children were considered to be the wife's.

Read Genesis 16:1-13. Hagar discovers that He was her hope soon after she fled her home. Thirsty, lonely, exhausted, she threw herself down by a spring in the wilderness.

No doubt she was downcast and disturbed. Where should she go now? What should she do next? Does the God of Abraham care about me? As Hagar thinks about this – she has a visitor.

Next we read that the angel of the Lord found her, and asks 'where are you coming from and where are you going?' Notice he knew right where to find her and he knew her name-Hagar. He also knew her occupation – servant of Sarah. He knew her heart-aches at home. What's more he knew her future. She was told to return home and deal with the problem, not to run away. She was probably headed back to Egypt.

Let's listen to her response. "Thou art a God who sees" (El Roi) Not only did God see where she was, He heard her cries.2 It's as if God is saying to her—what has hurt you? Where are you running?

Hagar needed hope - hope that things would change, hope that her life would get better, hope that there was a way out, hope of survival. She was alone, impoverished, pregnant. Yet she discovered she was not alone and she did have a future.

Many times when we're mistreated, we tend to run away – bury stuff!! Where does our healing of this hurt and distress begin? It can begin with the recognition of EL Roi – the God who sees. He was awake, aware and He saw it all. When we realize that God sees me—then we can say with Hagar, I have now seen the One who sees me.

Psalm 9 says, those who know His name (El Roi) will put their trust in You. You have not forsaken those who seek You.

There is another way to run to El Roi for hope! Maybe you have not run, but you may have a loved one who has left. They may have run away and shut themselves off from communication with you and God. You may have no idea what is happening in their lives. But El Roi sees and knows. He knows where they are and He sees it all – right now.

Now let's look at Genesis 21. Ishmael was mocking Isaac when he was weaned. Ishmael is around 14-15 years old and probably had some of Hagar's attitude. Ishmael is entitled to a share of the inheritance from Abraham. As the son of a slave, he can forego the inheritance in exchange for freedom. Sarah wants Isaac to be the sole heir. Abraham is distressed – Ishmael is his son too! So once again Hagar is sent away.

In verses 15-19, we find Ishmael slumped beneath a bush – feverish, dizzy, thirsty. The last of their water is gone. What could Hagar do this time? She begins to cry and wail out her grief. Was God unable to keep His promises? Was He unwilling to listen to her cries this time? Where was the God who sees when she needed him again! Hagar sobs. Remember the name Ishmael means "God hears" – it must have mocked her. She may have been saying, Did God really say that? Did God really promise that He would multiply my descendents?

Verse 17 says, God heard the boy crying. Then Hagar hears a voice calling, "Do not be afraid. God has heard the voice of the boy." God opened her eyes and she saw the very thing she had dreamed of – a well of water. Now the well was there all the time.

Hagar never saw it in the midst of her distress and problems. God upheld the word He had spoken to her in Genesis 16 – many years before.

Remember this thought when you think you have failed to find God's help or to receive an answer to your prayer. Ask El Roi, the God who sees you, to open your eyes to His working. Lord, open our eyes to see what You are doing.

Here's some personal hope for you.

From heaven The Lord LOOKS down and SEES all mankind; From His dwelling place He WATCHES all who live on earth - He who forms the hearts of all, who considers (OBSERVES) everything they do. But the EYES of the Lord are on those who fear Him, on those whose hope is in His unfailing love, to deliver and keep them......

Psalm 33:13-15,18 (NIV)

Circle all the words that refer to Him watching. Let your heart rejoice.

He will not let your foot slip – He who WATCHES over you will not slumber;…
The Lord WATCHES over you - The Lord is your shade at your right hand; the sun will not harm you by day, nor the moon by night… the Lord WATCHES over your life; The Lord will WATCH over your coming and going both now and forevermore.

Psalm 121:3,5,8 (NIV)

What does God watch?

1. over you
2. over your life
3. over your coming and going

The EYES of the Lord are everywhere, keeping WATCH on the wicked and the good.

Proverbs 15:3 (NIV)

The EYES of the Lord range throughout the earth to strengthen those whose hearts are fully committed to Him.

II Chronicles 16:9 (NIV)

Hope – trust – expect – be confident that God does see what is happening to you. He does hear your cry. And when you can not seem to find God's help or you can not seem to receive an answer to your prayers—ask El Roi to open your eyes to His work.

And for those who toil quietly as a caregiver, the one who helps her neighbor silently, those who give and give secretly, Matthew 6:34 says that God sees you also.

How have you experienced God's watchful eye??

Questions for Discussion and Reflection

1. Discuss how Hagar may have felt when the angel told her to return home.

2. Use Psalm 33:13-14, 18-19 (NIV) and circle all the words that have to do with look, see, watches.

3. Do the same with Psalm 121:3,5-8. Circle all the words that refer to Him watching.

4. Discuss how God has opened your eyes to see Him and His work.

Chapter 3

HOPE – WAITING ON GOD

*I wait for the Lord, my soul does wait,
and in His word do I HOPE.*

Psalm 130:5 (ASV)

Y ou know the word and the promise God gave to you. You know His character and He cannot lie.

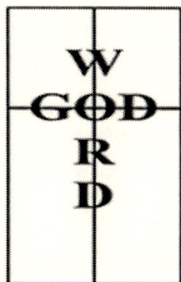

You have learned the things that can destroy your hope. You are anchored in Christ and you have asked Him to open your eyes to see Him and His work.

And you wait, and wait, and wait.

Let's look at Romans 15:4 and Hebrews 6: 17-18 again. Whatever was written in earlier times was written for our instruction and God desires to show us the unchangeableness of His purpose....

Many of us have found ourselves in God's waiting room. Sometimes we get tired of waiting for that "favorable" time. Sometimes we feel like giving up. Maybe you have even felt you can't believe anymore. You may even have thought that you must have heard God wrong or misunderstood Him. Maybe you have entertained the thought, "Did God really say that?"

-God's waiting room-

Let's picture God's waiting room. As you open the door and look for a seat, you notice the room is full. Looking across the room you spot Noah - waiting for rain. In the corner is Abraham – waiting for the promised land. On the other side of the room you see Job – weak and in pain – waiting for healing. Caleb is waiting for the land promised to him. David is there waiting for the promised kingdom. Jeremiah is there waiting for the restoration of the city. Then you see Joseph – who spent his prime years waiting. So if you are in the waiting room – you are in good company.

Noah may have spent the best part of one hundred twenty years building the ark. He was in the ark for one year and seventeen days. The ark floated for five months and then rested on a mountain for seven months.

Abraham was seventy-five when he went to Canaan. He was 81 when Ishmael was born and 100 when Isaac was born.

Caleb had to put his dream on hold as the ten spies gave a negative report. Forty years later he received the promise God had given him.

Job may have had a form of leprosy and elephantiasis. God's speech to him after waiting was not to expect to understand all the mysteries of God's creation and universe.

David was promised a kingdom and a line forever. Samuel anointed him a king at thirteen but he did not become king until he was thirty.

Jeremiah received a call from God at twenty. He spent his life preaching to get people to repent and turn to God.

Joseph was twenty-five years waiting.

-Joseph needed hope-

Let's take a closer look at Joseph – waiting. Genesis 37-45.

His childhood was blessed. He was the son of Rachael. He was his father's favorite. His father gave him a colored tunic when he was seventeen years old. His mother dies in childbirth and then his beloved grandfather, Isaac, dies also.

He thought God must have a special plan for him. But maybe he should have kept the dream to himself.

His brothers plotted against him and throw him into a pit. Then he is sold to traders in a caravan. He's only seventeen years old. When he gets to Egypt, he's sold to Potiphar. So much for his dream and the "purpose" God had for his life. He lost his family and maybe his dream.

The psalmist's feelings in Psalm 77 must have expressed Joseph's feelings – "In the day of trouble I sought the Lord; in the night my hand was stretched out with weariness; my soul refused to be comforted."

Joseph becomes a successful young man in Genesis 39. He finds favor in his master's eyes and the Lord was with him. Potiphar makes him the overseer of his house. Everything he owned is left in Joseph's charge.

All goes well until Potiphar's wife decides she wants him. His master ends up throwing him in jail on false charges.

Now he has lost his job. Another world has fallen apart for him. What happened to his dreams?

In Genesis 39 we find that once again the Lord is with him and gave him favor with the chief jailer.

Joseph is once again in a responsible position, trusted and useful. He is in charge of all prisoners and supervises everything inside the jail. After he meets the chief cupbearer and the baker and interprets their dreams, he must feel that things are looking up again.

He asks to be kept in mind when the cupbearer gets out of jail and all goes well with him.

The psalmist says in Psalm 34, the Lord is near the brokenhearted and saves those crushed in spirit.

After two full years Joseph is remembered by the cupbearer. Pharaoh sends for Joseph and he interprets the Pharaoh's dream of plenty and famine. Joseph even gives him suggestions on how to deal with this situation. Joseph is made ruler over Egypt (second only to Pharaoh.) He's given a signet ring, clothes, necklace, chariot, and a wife. He has had thirteen years of gain and loss – up and down. Joseph is now thirty years old and he has a new and much greater job. He has a wife and two sons.

Life is good!!!

- But what of his dreams as a teenager?
- Where is his original family?

Genesis 45 has the story of his family's restoration. He is restored with his brothers and eventually with his father, Jacob. They all go to Egypt to be with Joseph. He has spent many years waiting – 17 years to 42 years old. That's twenty-five years in waiting. His original family is restored and his dream is fulfilled. His response is encouraging to us. In Genesis 45: 8, he proclaims that it was not his brothers who sent him to Egypt but God. And in Genesis 50:20, Joseph believes that God meant all this for good.

***Let us hold unswervingly to the HOPE we profess,
for He who promised is faithful.***

Hebrews 10:23 (NIV)

-pits and pain-

Joseph was in a pit and a prison. Let's bring this closer to home for us. What pit or prison are you in? It's been said that you are either in the middle of one, coming out of one, or going into one!

Our hope while we're waiting can be in El Shaddai – the All-Sufficient One, the Almighty. Abraham was the first to hear of El Shaddai. In Genesis 17 we read, "I am God Almighty, I am El Shaddai. Walk before Me and be blameless and I will establish My covenant with you." In other words – I am everything to you. WOW – God says that! What hope!!

Kay Arthur in her book, the Peace and Power of Knowing God's Name, tells of running to her earthly father when she was hurt.1 He would pick her up and hold her – no matter how busy he was. So she visualized running to her heavenly Father with her hurts. As they opened the doors to the Throne Room, she saw El Shaddai sitting on the throne. He stopped what He was doing so she could run straight to Him. He picked her up and held her until the hurt was over. Sometimes it is easier for us to believe in God's power on a grand scale – creating and sustaining the universe – than to believe in His power to keep one single promise to us. Nothing can prevent El Shaddai, our Almighty God, from carrying out His plans and pouring His blessings on those who belong to Him.

Pain can be there in that pit – even confusion, struggle, difficulty – but God can use even these to bless us as long as we trust in Him. He will be "with us and give us favor". It's an interesting prophesy that was given to Joseph by his father Jacob. Genesis 49:25 states, " the God of your father who helps you, and by the Almighty (El Shaddai) who blesses you."

The word thwart means frustrate or turn back. Can anyone thwart the plans of God? NO! Isaiah 14:24 & 7 says, "The Lord of Hosts has sworn saying, surely, just as I have planned so it will stand. For the Lord of Hosts has planned, and who can frustrate it?" Even in Job 42 it states, "I know that Thou canst do all things, and that no purpose of Thine can be thwarted." Hold unswervingly to this hope. That means we are to seize, to hold fast, to retain hope without wavering.

Find rest, O my soul, in God alone; my HOPE
come from Him.
He alone is my Rock and my Salvation;
my Fortress,
I will not be shaken.

Psalm 62:5 (NIV)

There is a *trick* or *truth* thought here. Did God mean it or not? Let's see, although God spoke the universe into existence and hung the stars in space – even though He promised to help you – you think He can't or won't.

So what can you do while waiting....?

1. HOPE IN EL SHADDAI
2. HOLD UNSWERVINGLY TO THIS HOPE
3. FIND REST IN GOD – YOUR HOPE

Now is the time to replace the enemy's taunts and accusations with Scripture. IT IS WRITTEN. Whenever you start to question – open your Bible and speak the word out loud. Faith comes by hearing, so let your own ears hear the word from your mouth. At times like this, we do not need comforting senti-ments – we need the word of God.

Psalm 119:81 says, to wait on His word.....and Hope.

If you have not memorized or actively studied the word, you don't know or remember what He promised. So the question is – is it a trick or a truth? Did God mean what He said or not? God meant it for good – to save Joseph's family.

Peace will come while waiting as we give the problem to Him.

- Peace in aloneness
- Peace in provision
- Peace in a storm
- Peace in tears
- Peace in waiting

Peace while sitting down (like the multitude waiting to be fed) in a posture of trust. Quietly waiting to receive from Him.. Time is everything – even in waiting. Ecclesiastes 3:1 says, that to everything there is a season and a time.

The words to the southern gospel song, *FOUR DAYS LATE*, by C. Aaron Wilburn / Bill and Gloria Gaither are so encouraging and uplifting. The news came to Jesus that Lazarus was sick. Mary and Martha waited for Jesus to come, but Lazarus died and he had been buried for four days When Jesus arrived.

The song goes on to say that they felt all hope was gone and wondered Why Jesus had waited so long. But Jesus way is God's way and when He's Four days late, He's still on time. As they rolled the stone from the grave, Jesus cried for Lazarus to come forth.

So if you're fighting a battle and wonder where the Lord is, just remember that even if He is four days late – He's still on time.

Questions for discussion and reflection

1. What does God's covenant name – El Shaddai – God Almighty mean for your life?

2. How have you experienced God's almighty power working on your behalf?

3. Discuss if Joseph ever lost hope in his life situation.

4. Meditate on Psalm 13.

Chapter 4

Hope – gird your mind

Put on the breastplate of faith and love.....
and as a helmet the HOPE of salvation
(deliverance).

I Thessalonians 5:8 (ASV)

So let's see – you know what God has told you from His word and you know He cannot lie. You are anchored in the Rock and your knot of hope is tied firmly. And you are waiting for the promise to be fulfilled. But then it seems the battle begins in your mind.

Hope is not just for a few saints of God who have extra strong faith. II Corinthians 4:8-10 says, that we are pressed on every side—-but we are not in despair.

- afflicted – but not crushed
- perplexed – but not in despair
- persecuted – but not abandoned or forsaken
- struck down – but not destroyed

Some days our burdens seem too heavy and drag on us. We can feel crushed and in despair. Why didn't the Corinthian Christians feel this way? Verse 10 says that it was so the resurrection life of Christ could be seen in them. Verse 7 reminds us that the greatness of the power is of God and not from ourselves.

Our hearts can be lifted in the midst of dark circumstances. You can drown in one inch of water as well as ten feet of water. You can float in fifteen feet of water as well as five feet. That tells me that I can drown in small problems of life as well as the big problems. Or I can have hope in those big problems as well as the small ones. Again, hope is no respecter of circumstances. Hope does not really have much to do with what's going on around you.

I have known people to float in hope in some very dire circumstances. Early Christians were burned at the stake – but hoped in Jesus Christ. Parents continue to hope as their child is in the hospital. Many continue to hope even as their children have wandered from home and from God. Aids children in orphanages live in hope.

If we HOPE for what we do not see,
we eagerly wait for it with perseverance.

Romans 8:25 (NKJ)

-David needed hope-

David waited many years for his promised kingdom and experienced some heavy situations. For seventeen years he waited for Jehovah-Sabaoth, the Lord of Hosts. The prophet Samuel anointed David king when he was just a young teenager. I Samuel 16:13 says that the Spirit of the Lord came mightily on him from that day forward.

In I Samuel 17, we read that David was the youngest of his brothers. His brothers followed Saul as soldiers while David stayed home and tended the sheep. He was an untrained youth, fresh from the sheepfold. When he came to check on his brothers and heard the giant, Goliath, shouting at the armies of Israel, the word says in verse 26, that he asked "Who is this Philistine that he should taunt the armies of the living God?"

Hear the indignation in his voice. Then his brother Eliab says, "Why are you here?" Maybe his older brother did not like his younger brother to see him cowering before the giant. When the challenge arose, his brother attacked him verbally to discourage him. David goes on to say – "what have I done now?" Sounds like he's displeased his older brother before. Why is it that sometimes it's our family members who do not understand. It can be difficult when it seems your own family isn't standing with you and is against you.

David goes on to tell King Saul how he has slain a lion and a bear and says he will do the same to Goliath since he's taunted the armies of the Living

God. The king must have seen David differently than his brother did, because he put his armor on him.

Can't you picture David with Saul's full armor on? Saul who stood head and shoulders above the crowds – and David a young man. He knows he can not face Goliath this way. He probably could hardly move in the armor! So here he stands unarmed before a nine foot Goliath - a hardened warrior – who incidentally is also fully armed. David must have looked like a red-headed choir boy next to a heavy-weight champion.

Proverbs 18:10 says the Name of the Lord is a strong tower—run into it and be safe. Imagine a strong refuge you can run into when it's dark and the circumstances in life are at their darkest. When the battle is hot - run to Jehovah Sabaoth – the Lord of Hosts.

There are times in our lives when we look around and our first response is despair. The odds are against us and they seem overwhelming. The situation feels unbearable. This is the Name to run to when there is no other help. This is the name of God to use in times of conflict and warfare. Sabaoth means mass of angels or heavenly beings. Jehovah Sabaoth rules over angelic hosts – He is over the armies of heaven.

The first two instances of this name being used, are in I Samuel. It was a time of darkness and distress – the final decadent days of the Judges. It is the name David called on as he stood all alone against the giant enemy taunting him.

I Samuel 17:45-46 gives David's reply. "I come to you in the name of the Lord of Hosts, the God of the armies of Israel…..this day the Lord will deliver you up into my hands." Verse 47 goes on to say that the battle is the Lord's and He will deliver. It's like saying – It's not me you have to contend with – it is the Lord of Hosts-Jehovah Sabaoth. Isaiah 49 says, "I will contend with the one who contends with you…."

Jahweh Sabaoth occurs 240 times in the Hebrew reminding us that all of God's creation is under His rule and reign.

Ever wonder why the story emphasizes David's inability to do battle in the king's armor? I think it's because David would have been "credited" with the victory rather than the Lord of Hosts! So when we read in Psalm 46:1 & 7 that David says God is our refuge and strength, a very present help in trouble, therefore we will not fear…. the Lord of Hosts is with us….we can take David's word for it! He experienced it.

-Elisha has hope-

There is another example of Jehovah Sabaoth fighting overwhelming odds. In II Kings 6 we are told of how Elisha awoke one morning with his servant in a panic! A great army with horses and chariots had come by night and were surrounding the city. The servant's reaction seemed real – Oh no! what are we going to do?

But Elisha wisely answers in verse 16, "Do not fear, for those who are with us are more than those who are with them." He goes on to say, "O Lord open his eyes that he may see." The servant is astonished when he sees the horses and chariots of fire all around Elisha. What he saw was the army of heavenly hosts of Jehovah Sabaoth - the Lord of Hosts. That's good- but it gets even better.

Elisha asks God to close the eyes of the enemy. They do not realize that it's Elisha when he tells the soldiers that they have miscalculated and that they are in the wrong city. He then sends them in another direction.

Elisha then prays again for God to open the enemy soldier's eyes and they begin to realize that they are in the heart of enemy territory. These bands of soldiers never came again into the land of Israel.

This incident reminds us that no matter who is against us – God is for us!!!

Next time you feel that you are surrounded by an army of troubles and you're feeling overwhelmed – call on the Lord of Hosts for help. This is not a talisman to chant or a good luck charm. But God will intervene in His way and timing.

Gird your minds for action….
fix your HOPE completely on the grace
brought to you
at the revelation of Jesus Christ.

I Peter 1:13 (ASV)

What does it mean to gird your mind? The dictionary uses several synonyms – to encircle, to equip, to endow, to prepare for action.

David did not receive the promised kingdom after the battle with Goliath. Neither did he try to "work out" God's promise to him. In I Samuel 24, David cut off the edge of King Saul's robe while he was in a cave. He could have had Saul done away with right then. Instead he waits until Saul leaves the cave and then calls out to him and tells him what he has done and what he could have done. By this Saul knows and believes that the kingdom of Israel shall be in David's hands one day.

Let me ask once again – can anyone thwart the plans of the Lord of Hosts? No, surely just as He intended, so it happened and just as He planned, so it will stand.

-gird up-

Now let's look at some "How to's". In Daniel 1:8 it says that Daniel <u>made up his mind</u> so he was not enticed with the king's rich food and drink. In Daniel 10:12, he <u>set his heart</u> on humbling himself before God and obeying God. Daniel girded his mind to follow after God.

Romans 12:2 says, be transformed by the renewing of your mind to prove and know what the will of God is. And in Philippians 4:6-8 we are told that the peace of God will guard our heart and mind. We talked in chapter one about focusing on the grapes (promise of God) rather than concentrating on the giants (circumstances and problems) Philippians 4:8 tells us just how to do this. We are to think on these things - what is true, honorable, right, pure, lovely. Let your mind dwell on these things.

In Ephesians 6:10-18. we are told to put on the armor of God. Verse 10 says, finally (after everything is said and done) – you have done well faithful one. You are about to cross the finish line-your promise is almost here Be strong in the strength of His might, not your own – just like David did. Verse 11 says to stand firm –solid, unyielding, stand against. Against what? The strategies and deceits of the evil one – his schemes and wiles and devious plans. In short, his underhanded plot to destroy you.

Verse 12 goes on to say that our struggles (wrestle, to contend against, combat, strenuous effort) are against the rulers and powers (forces of darkness, spiritual forces of wickedness)). Doesn't this sound like what Elisha's servant came up against?

Ephesians 1 tells us that He is far above all rule, authority and power. Colossians 2 says that He disarmed rulers and authorities. I Peter 3:22 says the angel, authorities, and powers are subject to Him. Get the picture? We need to say Lord, open my eyes like You did Elisha's servant.

-helmet of hope-

The phrase "stand firm" is repeated three times in Ephesians 6. It means unyielding to pressure, solid, steadfast, final, unfluctuating. We can stand firm after we have the armor of God on. All the pieces of armor are important in order to stand firm. However, I want to talk in particular about the helmet of salvation in verse 17. Where else do we hear this phrase? Check again our verse from I Thessalonians 5:8. This talks about the helmet of hope.

Stop and think for a moment about the value of a helmet in battle and what it protects. We need to protect our mind, our brain, from the enemy. Once the helmet of hope is on—take up your sword—the Word of God. It is written..........

DON'T KEEP TAKING THE HELMET OFF! Whenever you slip off that helmet of hope, the enemy has access to harass your mind. Worrying does not move the hand of God. If you know how to worry, you know how to think on God's word. Worrying is thinking of the problem over and over. If you can think of the problem over and over, you can think of God's word - the answer - over and over.1 Use 3 x 5 cards and write scripture verses on them to read. Look at them over and over again. Read them aloud. Keep your helmet of hope on as you say – it is written. Hope will rise in your heart and mind.

And HAVING DONE ALL – STAND. When you have done all you know to do and all you can do –STAND FIRM.

So let's talk about some words of hope for your mind.

- Psalm 46:7 – the Lord of Hosts is with us.
- Psalm 84:12 – blessed is the man who trusts in the Lord of Hosts.

- Zachariah 1:3 – return to Me, that I may return to you says the Lord of Hosts.

If you don't actively read and hang on to these promises, the comfort can feel diluted. You think there is something in the Bible about God helping us, being with us, but you're not certain where it says this. You cannot put hope or trust in what you think – you need the word of God.

Questions for discussion and reflection

1. Can you remember times in your life when you felt like you were in a battle?

2. What one thing could you do today that would help you face further battles?

3. Using Philippians 4:8 as a guide, make a list of things to keep your mind on.

4. Pray morning and evening as in Psalm 55:17. don't let the enemy attack your thoughts in the morning or plant thoughts in your mind at bedtime.

Chapter 5

HOPE – the Great I AM

*Set your HOPE in God (confidence)
and do not forget the works of God.*

Psalm 78:7 (NKJ)

Let's look at the latitude and longitude of hope again.

```
W    +    GOD    =    W
O                     GOD } our "by-word"
R                     R
D                     D
```

The promise of God is the word of God and
He is faithful – He cannot lie.

There is a life story that Nicole Johnson relates – a story of stained glass redemption. She tells of a moving van that was to move all her possessions. As she opens the packages, many of her loved and cherished things are broken and damaged. She was particularly heartbroken to see that a treasured piece of stained glass was shattered beyond repair. Her friends gathered to pick up the pieces and throw them out for her. One friend took the broken pieces of stained glass and made a redesigned piece of art with them. As Nicole looked at it she realized that it was beautiful. Different but beautiful. Our lives can be like this piece of stained glass – broken, fragmented, wounded, shattered beyond repair. But don't throw away all the pieces. Instead cry and grieve and then bring these shattered pieces of your life to God. Let Him remake them into something new and beautiful.1

If God has already done this in your life, then remember and praise Him for what He has done. The Master Designer can not only create but He can recreate what has been shattered.

Blessed is he whose help is the God of Jacob, whose HOPE is in the Lord his God.

Psalm 146:5 (NIV)

The sacred name of God – Jahweh (Lord) means the Self-Existent One – the I AM. It's the name associated with the "works of God."

Jahweh occurs more than 6,800 times in the Old Testament. It appears in every book of the Bible except Esther, Ecclesiastes, and Song of Solomon. It was spoken aloud only by the priests in the temple.

Isaiah 43 says that "before Me there was no God formed. And there will be none after Me. I, even I, am the Lord. (Jahweh) and there is no Savior besides Me." Yahweh is the name most closely linked to God's redeeming acts in the history of His chosen people. We know God because of what He has done.

In Exodus 2:23-25, we read that God heard the groaning of His people. He remembered His covenant and took notice of them. Remember the incident in Exodus 3 of Moses and the burning bush. Moses said, I must turn aside and see this marvelous sight, why the the bush is not burned up. As he draws near and removes his sandals, God tells him, "I am the God of your father, the God of Abraham, the God of Isaac, and the God of Jacob.

In verse seven, Jahweh says, "I am aware of your sufferings" and again in verse 16, He says, "I am concerned about you and what has been done to you." He also tells Moses that He has seen the affliction of His people and 'SO I have come down to deliver them. Their cry has come before Me.'

Sometimes the Lord allows things and situations to get our attention from everyday life (like a burning bush), just to say to us …." I am your God." Acts 10:30 tells us that He is no respecter of persons.

This name (Jahweh) was a most holy glorious name. It gripped the Israelites with fear and awe – so much so that they would not even pronounce it. If they encountered it when copying the Old Testament, they would stop – take off their clothes – take a complete bath – put on clean clothes - and then….pick up a pen that had never been used to copy His name…Jahweh (Jehovah).

Humanists say "where is God? Who made Him? How did He come into existence?" The answer is in the name – Yahweh. He is the self-existent Creator who made the heavens and the earth. His name says, 'I always have been, I always am, and I always will be.'

Let's look again at Exodus 3. God gives Moses a mission and tells him, "I will be with you and this will be a sign to you that it is I who sent you. When you have brought the people out of Egypt, you will worship Me at this mountain." But Moses is concerned that the people will wonder who has sent him and how they will believe him.

Verse 14 says, " I AM WHO I AM" - tell them I AM has sent me to you. This is My name forever, this is My memorial name to all generations.

Have you ever wondered what these mysterious and strange words mean? I often wondered if Moses was bewildered by this statement - I AM that I AM. God is saying here to Moses that I AM the Self-Existent One. To me that means that He is telling Moses, I am everything and anything you will ever need.

Back in verse 16 & 17, God tells Moses to tell the people that, "I am concerned about you and what has been done to you –SO – I will give you favor!" These words should give you reason to hope. The God of yesterday, today and forever says to us today – I am your God. I have seen your affliction. I am aware of your sufferings. I have come down to deliver you from the power of the enemy.

Moses was concerned about all the what ifs. What if they do not believe me? He didn't speak well and he was a nomad! It does not matter who you are; it does not matter where you have been in your past. It does not matter where you find yourself now or where He will send you in the future. There is hope for you – for the call God has on your life.- for the mission and purpose He has for you. There are no what ifs – I AM will teach you what to say.

-I AM-

It's as if God is saying to us, nothing else matters. I am with you. You have everything you need. He is the eternal I AM. He is the Alpha and Omega. He is the same yesterday, today, and forever. He will be who He is and He will do what He has said He will do!!!

Perhaps your life has lots of what ifs. Maybe you're feeling the cold grip of fear and are wondering—

- What am I going to do if my husband dies?
- What if my spouses health continues to decline and I can no longer care for him?
- What if my health fails?
- What's going to happen if my children move away?
- What if I lost my job?
- What if I have no health insurance?

- How can I pursue the call of God-the mission of my life?

The great I AM says, "I will never leave you or forsake you; so we can confidently say – the Lord (Jehovah) is my helper. I will not be afraid" (Hebrews 13:15-16). What great hope for us!!

Let's bring this down even closer to us and read a few I AM'S These are some words Jehovah would say to you to bring hope.

I AM with you….I will keep you….
I will not leave you.

Genesis 28:15

I AM aware of your sufferings.

Exodus 3:7

I AM concerned about you
and what has been done to you.

Exodus 3:16

I AM THE Lord your healer.

Exodus 15:26

*I AM going to send an angel
to guard you along the way.*

Exodus 23:20

I AM the Lord who brought you out.

Exodus 29:46

I AM the Rose of Sharon, Lily of the Valley.

Song of Solomon 2:1

I AM with you.

Isaiah 43:5

I AM the One who wipes out transgressions.

Isaiah 43:25

I AM the Lord – is anything to difficult for Me?

Jeremiah 32:27

I AM in their midst.

Matthew 18:20

I AM the Bread of Life.

John 6:35

I AM the Light of the World.

John 8:12

I AM the good Shepherd.

John 10:11

I AM the Resurrection and the Life.

John 11:25

I AM says – I will never leave or forsake you.

Hebrews 13:5-6

I AM willing…..

Luke 5:13

What do you need today? What is God telling you that He is to you?

Blessed is the man who trusts in the Lord,
whose HOPE is in the Lord..

Jeremiah 17:7 (NKJ)

-hope in the Lord-

Let's take a look at Psalm 103:1-13. There are many things to hope in the Lord for in these verses.

- forgiveness for all your sins
- pardons all your iniquities – each one
- heals all your diseases – each one
- redeems your life from the pit and corruption
- crowns you with compassion and lovingkind-ness and mercy
- delights to bless you with good things
- satisfies your years with good things – neces-sity and desire – at your personal age and situation.
- works on behalf of those oppressed for justice
- slow to anger
- gracious and compassionate
- loving
- doesn't deal with us according to our sins

(that should bring you hope)

Take time to praise Yahweh – what a hope we have! Here's more in case you feel the need for more hope from the promises associated with God's name – Yahweh – I AM.

- *Prov. 3:26* – He will keep you from falling. (I Samuel 2:9 says that He keeps the feet of His godly ones.)
- Proverbs 18:10 – Run into His name and be safe. The name Jahweh is a strong tower.
- Deuteronomy 28:9,12 – the Lord will bless the work of your hands v.13 says to listen and observe His commands carefully.

- Psalm 32:10 – thanks to Yahweh for surrounding me with unfailing love.
- Psalm 34:18 – Yahweh is close to the brokenhearted.
- Numbers 6:24-27 (AMP) – Yahweh is used three times in this section.

This is a beautiful benediction to pray over your family.

Yahweh bless you and keep you (watch, guard)
Yahweh make His face shine on you
and be gracious to you.
(be kind, merciful to you, approve
of you and give you favor)
Yahweh lift His countenance
on you and give you peace.
(peace in your heart and your life)

A final word here of hope for you can be found in Psalm 138:8.

The Lord will accomplish what concerns me;
Thy lovingkindness, O Lord, is everlasting.
do not forsake the works of Thy hands.

Questions for discussion and reflection

1. Pray this benediction from Numbers 5:24-27 over your family.

2. Make a list of the I AM verses that connect with you.

3. Discuss how God used an incident (burning bush) to get Moses' attention from everyday life as a nomad, to listen to what He had to say.

4. Meditate on Psalm 9. Think about the different ways we can be needy and poor. Then connect these thoughts with verses 9 and 10.

Chapter 6

HOPE - remembrances

I remember my affliction and my wandering,
the bitterness and the gall…,
yet this I call to mind,
and therefore I have HOPE:
because of the Lord's great love
we are not consumed,
for His compassions never fail.
they are new every morning;
great is your faithfulness.

Lamentations 3:19-23(NIV)

There is an interesting sign I saw recently that said GODISNOWHERE. At a quick glance most in the group read this as God is no where. God has abandoned me. However, one person in the group saw this as God is now here!! So what can we do to remind ourselves that God is here – now in our circumstances? The key to remembering, is to remember what He has done in the past.

Circle the phrase "call to mind" in Lamentations. Call to mind what? Remember what? - God's love, His compassion, His faithfulness.

Philippians 3:13 says to forget those things which are behind. Is this a contradiction? NO. We need to forget things like bitterness, affliction, failures, guilt……. but we do need to call to mind what God has done.

- Deuteronomy 4:9 says do not forget what your eyes have seen.
- Deuteronomy 2:7 – do not forget what God has provided – You have not lacked a thing.

The Israelites were provided with water, quail, manna, their sandals did not wear out, their enemies were defeated, diseases were healed. They were to remember these things.

- Deuteronomy 4:31 – God will not fail you, nor destroy you, nor forget the covenant with you.
- Deuteronomy 8:2 - you shall remember all the way the Lord your God has led you.

We need to remember and call to mind the things God has done for us.

Sometimes we feel like we lose hope in "stormy weather". We can feel like we won't survive the gales of life that are lashing at us. But one secret to surviving the storm is to remember all the times that God has led you in the past.

Lee Williams from Kentucky lost his family in a tragic fiery bus accident but shared that there are three ways to make it through tragedy.

1. God
2. Memories
3. Heaven

He also shared his custom of Job 1:5 – calling his children by name and putting a hedge around them each day. He said that the memories kept him going on the hardest of days. The memories of all the good times, the memories of what God has done in the past, and the promise of heaven all kept him going.

Remember and think on God's faithfulness. Sometimes the storm continues in our life – even when you've prayed for help and deliverance. Is God indifferent? Doesn't He answer prayer? Where is He?

Start to remember all the times God has delivered you and answered your prayers. Remember where to put your hope. He calms the storm! I remember His great love and compassion, His faithfulness – therefore I have hope.

For I know the plans I have for you,
declares the Lord,
plans for welfare and not for calamity,
to give you a future and a HOPE.

Jeremiah 29:11 (ASV)

Yahweh Tsuri means the Lord my Rock. There is no better word than "Rock" to describe God's permanence, protection, and faithfulness. His purpose and plans remain firm throughout history.1

- Psalm 144:1 says, Praise be to the Lord my Rock, who trains my hands for war, my fingers for battle.
- Psalm 144:2 says, my lovingkindness and my fortress, my stronghold, my deliverer, my shield – in Him I take refuge.

Rocks provide shade, shelter, and safety. They were used to construct altars, temples, and city walls. Stones were used to commemorate important events in Israel's history. God gave commandments to Moses on tablets of stone. The word rock emphasizes His enduring faithfulness.

Hannah said in I Samuel 2:2, "There is no Rock like our God."

Read what David said in II Samuel 22:2-4. The Lord is my Rock, my fortress, my deliverer; my God is my rock, in whom I take refuge. My shield, my salvation, my stronghold.

King Saul made himself David's enemy many times. David had no need to get even – He knew that God his rock would deal with Saul. He believed that the promises God had made to him were as solid as the rock he stood on.

Few of us have enemies with a big "E" like David did, most of ours are the small "e" type.

Isaiah 26:3-4 says to trust in the Lord forever, for the Lord is the Rock eternal. Psalm 62:1-2 state that He alone is my rock and Salvation. I will not be shaken.

So what are you facing today that frightens or shakes you?

- Illness?
- Job loss?
- Trouble at home?
- Difficulties at work?

No matter how out of control your life may seem, make a decision to keep your eyes glued on Jesus. Recommit yourself to not only hearing the word – but building your life on it. Build on the Solid Rock!!!

- altars-

Let's talk about stones and altars now. There were many altars built in the Old Testament. Each altar was built for a reason – a specific significance.

1. Noah in Genesis 8 built an altar after the flood – "an offering by fire to the Lord" God approved – "smelled the soothing aroma.
2. Abraham in Genesis 12:7 – built an altar to the Lord after God called him to go to another land and blessed him. And in Gen. 12:8. He built an altar and called upon the name of the Lord – the Everlasting God. In

Gen. 22:9 he built an altar to Jehovah Jirah – God provides.

3. Isaac in Genesis 26:25 built an altar and called upon the name of the Lord. God had given him blessing and promise.

4. Jacob in Genesis 35:1 & 7, God told him to make an altar to God who appeared to him.

5. Moses in Exodus 17:15 built an altar named the Lord is my Banner. In Exodus 24, he built an altar with twelve pillars for the twelve tribes of Israel. He wrote down all the words of the Lord.

6. Joshua in Joshua 6:24, built an altar to the Lord – the God of Israel.

7. Gideon in Judges 6:24, built an altar to the Lord and named it the Lord is Peace after he had seen the Lord face-to-face.

8. Samuel in I Samuel 7:17. built an altar to the Lord.

9. Saul even built an altar to the Lord in I Samuel 14:35.

10. David built several altars to the Lord. In II Samuel 24:25, he built an altar and offered peace offerings. God was moved by entreaty and held the plague back. And in I Chronicles 21:26, he built an altar to the Lord and He answered him.

11. Elijah in I Kings 18:32. built an altar in the name of the Lord before the Baal worshippers.

Each altar had a reason. For some altars it was an answer to prayer, some altars signified that God had met them. Some altars were to agree on a covenant with God. Deuteronomy 8 said to 'remember all the way which the Lord your God has led you'. And in Deut. 27:2 it says to 'write on stones the words of the law'.

Let's look at the life of Joshua. We'll start with Numbers 13. The spies were sent out to see what the land was like, whether the people who lived in it were strong or weak, whether they were few or many. Was the land "good or bad"? Was the land "fat or lean"? Were there trees in it or not? And they were to bring back some of the fruit of the land. In verse 27, the spies tell Moses and Aaron, this is the fruit of the land. It was Joshua and Caleb in chapter 14 that said it's a good land. They were looking at the fruit and not the giants.

In Deuteronomy we see that Moses' time on earth is ending. He calls Joshua to present himself at the tent of meeting. God was going to commission Joshua to take Moses place as the leader of the Israelites. In verse 23, God commissions Joshua and tells him to be strong and courageous, for he will bring the sons of Israel into the land that God has promised them and He will be with him. Now that's hope for the future.

In Deuteronomy 34, Moses dies and Joshua is now in charge. He is filled with the spirit of wisdom, for Moses had laid his hands on him.

So now we come to Joshua 1. God charges Joshua with the instruction to cross over this Jordan.

He tells him that every place his foot treads, He has given it to him. The hope promise that God speaks to Joshua is – "I will be with you and I will not fail or forsake you". Joshua is told to be strong and courageous – not to give in to fear and doubt. He is further instructed to not turn from what God's Word says to the right or to the left, so that he might have success wherever he goes.

The task for Joshua was similar to what Moses had faced. He is to cross the Jordan as Moses crossed the Red Sea. There is unknown land and challenge ahead! Nothing tries courage as much as the unknown!! God once again tells Joshua to be strong and courageous.

At this time, Joshua sends the spies to go look at Jericho. And in Joshua 3, the Israelites are about to cross Jordan. The Jordon River stands in the way - barring the entrance to the promised land. The river is at flood stage. Only God can intervene. So they consecrate themselves to God knowing that He is about to do wonders among them. As the Lord encourages Joshua by these words, "I will be with you", he knows that a promise is about to be realized. The promise that God gave is about to take place.

Joshua is to tell the priests to carry the ark of the covenant to the edge of the waters and to stand still in the Jordan river. Note that the water did not part or dry up until the priests feet were in the water. Joshua assures them that the living God – El Chay – the One true God of miracle and power will prove His presence to them by driving out the inhabitants of the land. He will conquer their enemies so that they will know He is the Living God.

I find it interesting that the priests had to step into the Jordan water before it was cut off. The word says they stood and crossed on dry ground. It was not squishy mud. There was no trickle of water. There was no soft sandy ground to sink into. The priests stood firm on dry ground and it remained dry until all the nation had finished crossing the Jordan. They knew the Living God was among them.

-Joshua's altar-

The rest of the story is in Joshua 4. I call this the story of the memorial stones. After the Israelites crossed the Jordan, Joshua had twelve men – one from each tribe – take up stones from the Jordan river bed where the priests were standing. They were to carry them over to where they were staying and pile them together.

This was to be done so that in the days to come when the children would say, "what do these stones mean'? – they could tell them of how God had cut off the waters of the Jordan for them to cross over. The stones were to be a memorial to the sons of Israel, a reminder of what God had done for them.

It's interesting that God told Joshua to do this. It seems that we too often forget what God has done for us. He knows we need to be reminded of what He has done. It's not only our children who need to remember what God has done – we need to remember what He has done.

Just as God drove out the Canaanites, Hittites and Hivites – He can drive out your enemies. The enemies of addiction, fear, sense of hopelessness and He can replace them with freedom. Take that first step into the water yourself. You may have to stand firm in the middle until the work is finished.

Take a few minutes to think of the times God has rescued you in the past. We need to find ways to remember what He has done for us. Remember how He has delivered you and helped you.

> ***Remember your word to your servant,***
> ***for You have given me HOPE.***

Psalm 119:49 (NIV)

This wonderful chapter in Psalms has many references to the law, the word, the decree. There are five times here that we are told to put our hope in the word. Look especially arc these verses.

- v. 43 – I put my hope in your laws
- v. 49 – Remember your word to me
- v. 74 – I've put my hope in your word
- v. 81 – I've put my hope in your word
- v. 114 – I have put my hope in your word
- v. 147 – I put my hope in your word
- v. 89 – says that His word is eternal – firm

It's in His word that we put our hope – not on feeling, emotion, or even circumstances. IN HIS WORD!! These blessings come not by wishing, but by sinking your roots into God. Spend time in prayer and reading His words to you. Hold fast to His commands.

-memorial stones-

We may need to make memorial stones in our lives for what God has done for us in the past. They will increase your hope that as He has helped you in the past – He can help you again. Stones of when we've crossed over a difficult - even impossible time in our lives. Stones to remind us that He has delivered us from sin. Memorial stones of when He has provided for us. Stones of when He has planted our feet on firm ground.

I would like to suggest we make some remembrance stones to help us remember what He has promised us in His word for our present situations. What word has God spoken to you to encourage you to know that He is by your side? What words of comfort has He given you to remind you that He will fulfill His word to you? You might underline the word, you might write it on cards. You could paint the word on a stone and set it out in your kitchen to be a reminder of what God has spoken to you -a HOPE remembrance stone.

- When tragedy comes – and it will,
- When the world around us trembles and shakes – and it will
- We will not be shaken.

The Lord is our Rock and will be there – giving us rest and peace.

Remember….Remember what God has done!

Questions for discussion and reflection

1. Make a remembrance stone for yourself. Paint a verse on it.

2. Discuss how the memorial stones at the Jordan River could affect the next generation.

3. How might the priests feel as they stepped their feet into the river?

4. Read Psalm 119. Notice all the verses that use the word law, decree, or word in them.

Chapter 7

HOPE – for your future

HOPE deferred makes the heart sick,
but a desire fulfilled is a tree of life.

Proverbs 13:12 (ASV)

What about your future – your family? What have you been holding on to God for? How do you deal with the hurt and the heartsickness when your hope is postponed or delayed? How do you calm yourself when you are feeling "heart sick"?

Do you run, hide, ignore, counter attack? Do you keep so busy you don't have time to think? Do you put on a false face of "happy, happy, happy"?

We need to take some time to gather up our fears – small and large - and take them to the Lord. This is a short list of some concerns and fears that you may have.

- fear of failure
- marriage
- rejection
- illness
- financial loss or indebtedness
- accidents
- flying
- aging
- public speaking
- health
- death
- job
- children
- decisions

Ask God to deliver you from these fears and to give you new hope!

Listen to the words of the song God on the Mountain by Tracy Dartt.1

Life is easy when you're on the mountain,
And you've got peace of mind like you've never
known;
But when things change and you're down in the
valley,
Don't lose faith for you're never alone.

And the god on the mountain is still God in the
  valley,
When things go wrong, He'll make them right;
And the God in the good times is still God in the
  bad times,
The God of the day is still God of the night.

...there is HOPE for Israel in spite of this.

Ezra 10:2 (NKJ)

Have you been unfaithful to God? Have you done
wrong? Have you tried to manipulate like Sarah did
to fulfill some promise that God gave you? Have you
been feeling loaded with guilt? Do you have uncon-
fessed sin in your life?

Let's look at the exiles in Ezra. In chapter
eight, Ezra journeys from Babylon to Jerusalem.
King Darius had decreed that the house of God in
Jerusalem was to be rebuilt. Ezra proclaims a fast
– that they might humble themselves before God. So
the people fasted and sought God – then they came
to Jerusalem.

Some of the princes approached Ezra to let him
know that many of the people had not separated
themselves from the "ites" of the land. In Ezra 9:5-
15 we read a prayer of confession. Ezra tells God that
he is embarrassed and ashamed to lift his face to God
because of the iniquities of the people. He says they
have forsaken His commandments.

Chapter 10 goes on to tell how they made recon-
ciliation to God. It started with praying, confession,

weeping and seeking God. Now we have our key Hope verse – in spite of this – there is hope for us.

Why is there hope? Because God is faithful to forgive those who seek Him and repent of their ways. Let this be an encouragement for us to do the same. Remember the hope verse from chapter one – for whatever was written in earlier times – was written for our instruction, that through perseverance and encouragement of the Scriptures – we might have hope.

We can learn from the people in Ezra's time. If you're carrying around sin – there is still hope for you. Repent, confess and seek God. He is the same today as yesterday and will forgive and cleanse you too.

What encouragement from the scripture to know that even if you have fallen short, missed the mark, maybe haven't lived up to the life God intended for you, there is still hope for you in spite of this. Now we need to move on for what God has for us.

For I HOPE in Thee, O Lord, Thou wilt answer, O Lord my God..

Psalm 38:15 (ASV)

Doesn't this verse feel like peace! So after hope is deferred and making us heartsick and "in spite of this" – let's look at peace.

-Gideon needed hope-

Yahweh Shalom means the Lord of Peace. Next we will look at the life of Gideon in Judges. Here we find that the sons of Israel had done what was evil in the sight of the Lord. For seven years they were given into the hand of the Midianites. Because the Midianites were so oppressive, the Israelites lived in shelters in the mountains, caves and strongholds.

When the Israelites tried to sow their wheat, the Midianites would come out and camp against them. They would destroy the produce that was coming up. So Israel was brought very low and cried out to the Lord.

The angel of the Lord appeared to Gideon while he was threshing wheat in a wine press. He was threshing it here in order to save it from the Midianites. Now, I'm not a farmer but I do know that you do not thresh in a winepress! You usually need open air and a good breeze, because you're separating the heavier grain from the lighter chaff. Gideon was working in secret and in the dark. The Angel of the Lord announces that "The Lord is with you".

Gideon's reaction is that if the Lord is with us – why has all this happened to us? And where are all the miracle which our fathers told us about? The Lord has abandoned us – GODISNOWHERE. The Lord tells him to go in the strength he has and save Israel from the Midianites. Gideon feels how can he deliver Israel? He is the least of the least. The Lord tells him again that He will be with him and Gideon will defeat the Midianites. Gideon wants a sign that this is so......

Gideon then prepares a kid and some bread for the angel and brings it to him. The angel says to put it on a rock and pour out the broth. Gideon does this. The angel of the Lord touched it with his staff and fire sprang up from the rock and consumed it. Then the angel vanished from his sight.

In verse 22, when Gideon saw this he said, now I have seen the angel of the Lord face-to-face. The Lord said to him – Peace, do not be afraid. Gideon built an altar to the Lord there and called it "the Lord is Peace". Whatever happened from this point on, Gideon could look back at this moment in time when Jehovah-Shalom had said, "Peace."

-our peace-

This is a great incident of God working in the Bible. Now let's bring this thought closer to us. Do you ever feel surrounded by your troubles? Do you ever wonder where God is in the midst of your hurt and worry? Have you ever wondered where the miracles are that you have heard about?

It's right that Gideon named the altar, the Lord is Peace. This story reminds us that true peace comes only from God. We can not base our peace on circumstances and situations in life. We can not even let our peace be centered in another person – spouse of friend.

Our peace cannot depend on:

- plenty of food to eat
- a balanced checkbook
- a retirement account
- a good education
- a perfect marriage
- a fantastic job
- a healthy body

Sometimes the Lord allows situations in our lives that strip away our surface peace. We can be distressed and turn to spouses or friends and find – it's not helping. Real peace comes only from God. Ephesians says that He is our Peace. Once you understand this – you can worship Him and have peace, no matter what storms come your way.

If you have been feeling troubled and restless – take a look inside. What's stealing your peace? What's making you anxious and frustrated? Have you made compromises that you know are wrong? Have you been too busy and feel your peace eroded?

Where do you run when you need peace?

- A friend?
- The nearest telephone?
- Your spouse?
- Your mother?
- TV?
- Food?

Run to Him – the Lord of Peace, the Prince of Peace. If in need of peace – hold on to these verses:

Do not be anxious about anything,
but in everything,
by prayer and petition, with thanksgiving present
your request to God.
and the peace of God, which transcends
all understanding, will guard
your hearts and your mind in Christ Jesus.

Philippians 4:6-7

You will keep in perfect peace him whose mind is
steadfast, because he trusts in you.

Isaiah 26:3

Peace, I leave with you; My peace I give to you;
not as the world gives, do I give to you. Let not
your heart be troubled, nor let it be fearful….
These things I have spoken to you, that in
Me you may have peace. In the world you have
tribulation, but Take courage;
I have overcome the world.

John 14:27; 16:33

Many years ago I compiled a list of scripture verses that use the phrase' He is able'. They are listed here for your encouragement. These verse bring hope and can help relight your peace.

Hope Builders – He is able

1. II Timothy 1:12 – I am sure (positively persuaded) that HE IS ABLE to safely guard (protect, defend, watch over, keep) all that I have given Him until the day of His return.
2. II Corinthians 9:8 – GOD IS ABLE to make it up to you by giving (all grace, every favor and blessing) you everything you need and more, so that there will not only be enough for your needs, but plenty left over to give joyfully to others.
3. Hebrews 2:18 - Since He Himself has been through suffering and temptations, He knows what is is like when we suffer and are tempted, and HE IS WONDERFULLY ABLE to help us. (to run, to assist, to relieve us)
4. Hebrews 7:25 – HE IS ABLE to save completely (to the uttermost, perfectly, finally) all who come to God through Him.
5. Jude 24 – HE IS ABLE to keep you from slipping and falling away, and to bring you sinless (unblemished, blameless, faultless) and perfect, into His glorious presence with mighty shouts of joy.
6. Romans 4:21 – GOD WAS WELL ABLE to do anything He promised (and mighty to keep His word).
7. Philippians 3:21 – HE IS ABLE even to subdue (transform, fashion over exert power) all things unto Himself.

8. Daniel 3:17 – Our GOD IS ABLE to deliver us, and He will.
9. Ephesians 3:20 – HE IS ABLE to do far more than we would ever dare to ask or even dream of – infinitely beyond our highest prayers, desires, thoughts or hopes.
10. Matthew 9:28-29 – Believe you that I AM ABLE to do this? They said, yes Lord, and He said according to your faith be it unto you.

There is HOPE for your future declares the Lord, your children shall return to their own land.

Jeremiah 31:17 (NKJ)

-hope for your children-

This is a wonderful verse of hope for your future. Many of you have prayed for your children – there is hope for your future. Hold on to Him and have peace.

Kathy Benson from Emerge Ministries told of an incident in her life in which she learned to trust God for the future of her children. At the time of the birth of her second child, she was busy in college, busy in church ministry, busy with her daughter and husband. She had the timing of the birth all figured out in her mind. She knew her mother-in-law would be there to help, knew when the nursery would be ready and when her college paper would be finished. She had it all well planned. However, the baby was premature. She thought "God, what of all my plans? I'm not ready yet." Later she was to find that God always knows what is best for us. The doctor told her that the umbilical cord had been around the baby's neck and that if he had been born "on time" – he probably would have died. God had a future for her and her son – and later her grandson.

Trust that God knows where you are and what you need.

Now let me suggest a tangible project for you to consider. We're told to be doers of the word and not hearers only. Sometimes we need to put feet to our prayers. Do you know someone who is feeling one of the fears listed in this chapter? What would you want to say to encourage them if this were the last letter or word of hope you could give them. Let me suggest that you write a note to them and share a word of hope.

Questions for discussion and reflection

1. Be a doer of the Word, write a note of hope and encouragement to someone this week.

2. Plan a special time of prayer and fasting.

3. Discuss how Gideon may have felt when the angel of the Lord appeared to him.

4. Reread Philippians 4:6-8.

Chapter 8

HOPE – does not disappoint

HOPE does not disappoint,
because the love of God has been poured out
within our hearts
by the Holy Spirit who was given to us.

Romans 5:3-5 (NKJ)

It has been said that God's people live by promises – not by explanations! So don't lose heart – hope does not disappoint. Your life can not be lived by looking backwards. Look back at good memories and what God has done. Then we must again place our hands firmly on the "plow' and push forward.

Plowing a straight even row requires keeping your eye fixed on something ahead. A farmer doesn't plow his field continually looking backward. He sets his vision straight ahead and heads the tractor at that fixed point. Likewise we need to look ahead at the promise of God and move forward.

The farmer also checks his rows after planting to see if it's sprouting. That's hope. In I Corinthians 9, we read that the plowman plows in hope and the thresher threshes in hope. We can check to see if the seed of our promise is sprouting. Remember that Jesus said in Luke 18:1, that at all times we ought to pray and not lose heart and faint. Do not give up – keep hope – keep praying.

Read II Corinthians 4:16 from the Amplified Bible. Do not be discouraged (utterly spiritless, exhausted, wearied out through fear). Do not lose heart in doing good.

There is a wonderful chapter in the Women of Faith book, <u>Irrepressible Hope</u> written by Nicole Johnson. She retells the story of Dorothy in the Land of Oz. She clicked her ruby slippers three times and said, "there's no place like home". She had awakened to a world of munchkins, scarecrows, wicked witches – and all she wanted to do was go home.1

We can find ourselves in a place we don't understand and we want so much to get to a safe comfortable place again. We long for peace and a place where people care about us. We want to be surrounded by love and care.

That place is hope. Hope says that what you see with your eyes is not all there is. But hope has no strength of it's own. We can not hope in hope. So the strength of hope is what we hope in.

If we hope for a promotion and the boss favors someone else – we're crushed. But if we hope in

God's provision for our lives – our hope is in something strong enough to sustain us. When we feel out of control, we hope someone is in control and He assures us that He is looking after us. We want to close our eyes, click our ruby slippers and say, there's no place like hope – there's no place like hope – there's no place like hope. -hope does not disappoint-

There was a time when my teenage grandson was very depressed. He began dressing in dark colors and it was difficult to get him out of bed. He seemed to live in his room without caring about anything. His smile was gone. As his depression deepened, we began to be greatly concerned for him.

As we prayed for him, we talked about the scripture verse in Proverbs 29:18, 'without a vision the people perish'. We encouraged him to get a vision for his life – to consider what he would like to be doing five and ten years from now. My heart's cry was that God would free him from this depression…. "and hope does not disappoint". Today he is a Christian father with two children of his own. He always has a smile and sparkle about him.

Return to the stronghold O prisoners who have HOPE, this very day I am declaring that I will restore double to you.

Zachariah 9:12 (ASV)

The name of the Lord is a strong tower – run and be safe. The Strong Tower name to look at next is Jehovah Raah (Jahweh Roi) The Lord is my Shepherd.2 Now here is the ultimate hope.

We are told in Psalm 95 to come and worship and bow down. kneel before the Lord our Maker; for He is our God and we are the sheep of His pasture, the sheep of His hand.

Positive thinking can be good but do not let it become a belief in yourself. 'You can do it – just think right.' Because sometimes I can't do it, some-times I'm not strong enough. Sometimes I feel like a ….sheep. Rather than believing in myself, I would rather turn my hope to a God who says that He is my Shepherd and I shall not want. God designed us to be what we are – so we would see our need for Him.

The Lord tells us in Ezekiel 34 that He will feed His flock, He will lead them to rest. He will seek the lost and bring back the scattered. He will bind up the broken and strengthen the sick. What hope!!!

Even in Revelation 7 we read that the Lamb in the center of the throne shall be our Shepherd and He shall guide us to springs of the water of life and God Himself shall wipe away every tear from our eyes.

Let's take a look at Psalm 23. I've often wondered how our lives would change if we really believed that God's goodness and kindness (mercy) would follow us all the days of our life. That's hope!!!!

-positive hope-

Here's a list of some wonderful things to hope for – all in Psalm 23.

relationship	refreshment	purpose
supply	healing	testing
rest	guidance	protection
faithfulness	consecration	security
discipline	abundance	eternity
hope	blessing	

Let me show you these in the Psalm itself.

The Lord is my Shepherd
>   *that's relationship*

I shall not want
>   *that's supply*

He maketh me to lie down in green pastures.
>   *that's rest*

He leadeth me beside the still water.
>   *that's refreshment*

He restoreth my soul
>   *that's healing*

He leadeth me in the paths of righteousness
>   *that's guidance*

For His name sake
    that's purpose

Yea, though I walk through the valley of the
    shadow of death
    that's testing

I will fear no evil.
    that's protection

For Thou art with me
    that's faithfulness

Thy rod and Thy staff they comfort me,
    that's discipline

Thou preparest a table before me in the presence
    of my enemies
    that's hope!

Thou anointest my head with oil,
    that's consecration

My cup runneth over.
    that's abundance

Surely goodness and mercy shall follow me all
    the days of my life.
    that's blessing

And I will dwell in the house of the Lord.
    that's security

Forever.
> *that's eternity.*

Continue in faith firmly established and steadfast, not moved away from HOPE.....

Colossians 1:23 (ASV)

Here are some wonderful scriptures with the phrase - I am persuaded. These are included for your encouragement to not move away from hope.

***I am persuaded** that He is able to keep that which I have committed to Him.*

II Timothy 1:12

***I am persuaded** that .....nothing shall be able to separate us from the love of God.*

Romans 8:39

***I am fully persuaded** that what He had promised, He was able to perform.*

Romans 4:21

Set our HOPE on He who will yet deliver us.

II Corinthians 1:10 (ASV)

Look at Daniel in Daniel in chapter 6. In verse 26 Daniel proclaims that God is the living God who endures forever – He delivers and rescues and performs signs and wonders. But Daniel had a trip to the lion's den before this happened.

When you feel the farthest away from your hope promise – you could really be the closest. God has put us on this earth for a purpose. Daniel was there for a purpose. We must be steadfast and obedient like Daniel to see hope realized.

Daniel was a foreigner in the country and made it to the top leadership. King Darius appointed 120 satraps over the kingdom. These men were account-able to three commissioners – Daniel was one of them. He became distinguished among all of them. Then jealousy rears its ugly head. The other commis-sioners and satraps want to get rid of Daniel. That's 122 to one.

Ever had that happen to you when God has given you favor? A word here of advice – don't look at people. It's the adversary that comes to kill and destroy. He wants to destroy your hope – the hope of anything in your life ever changing.

-Daniel's hope-

These men find a way to trap Daniel. They present what seems like a good plan to King Darius, and the king signs the document. The petition said that no one can make a petition to god or man. The only peti-tions could be to the king.

Now Daniel knows that the document was signed. What did he do? He continued kneeling on his knees three times a day, praying and giving thanks to God. He was steadfast and faithful. Daniel did not run to the king for help or with explanations of what he was doing. He was more concerned about God's name than he was in promoting his own name in the high palace before the king.

Daniel KNEW the document was signed when he entered his prayer room to pray with the windows facing Jerusalem. But he was still praying - still hoping – still standing firm. That means remain, abide, live, persevere – still. He didn't take offense at words. He didn't allow himself to be distracted. He still kept making his petitions to his God.

There seems to be a lot of discouragement in the churches today. I believe it's a scheme of the enemy to get us distracted from what God has said to us. We can become discouraged by health issues, finances, problems, rumors and so many things. Daniel could have been discouraged. He went from top leader in the kingdom to the lion's den.

This should be THE END for him. He could have given up, but he was spared because he trusted God. Psalm 20 tells us that the Lord will save and He will answer when they call.

Daniel was not only cast into the lion's den but a stone was rolled over the mouth of the den He was "sealed" in this situation. Nothing could be changed – he was trapped. He might as well accept the situation and give up. That's what some people might have said – but there is more to this story.

The next morning King Darius rushes to the lion's den to see if Daniel has lived. He asks the question 'Has your God whom you constantly serve, been able to deliver you from the lion's?' God had sent an angel to shut the lion's mouths. This showed Daniel to be innocent before God and before the king. There was no injury found in him, because he trusted in God. Daniel stood firm and was delivered and rescued. He saw signs and wonders.

-stand in hope-

Do you need restoration instead of desolation? Do you need gladness instead of mourning? Do you desire good news instead of affliction? Do you need freedom from being brokenhearted? Do you need the mantle of praise instead of a spirit of fainting and giving up?

Let me ask what den you are trapped in today.

- discouragement
- division
- deception

Does it feel like a stone is in front of the den and you will never get out? Are you feeling that since you serve the King you shouldn't be in this position? Are you feeling that God can not use you anymore? These are lies and deceptions of the enemy. When the Lord fills you with the Holy Spirit, deception is broken.

II Thessalonians 2:15-17 tells us to stand firm and to hold on to what you have been taught. Jesus Himself will give you comfort and hope and strengthen you. Let me encourage you that in having done all – to stand firm. (Ephesians 6:13)

Questions for discussion and reflection

1. Memorize Psalm 23.

2. Why do you think Daniel went into his room to pray when he knew the decree was signed?

3. What do you think Daniel might have prayed knowing the other commissioners and satraps were listening?

Chapter 9

HOPE – open my eyes Lord

⌒

We have read how to "fix" our position in life with God's word and God's character. We know God sees and knows where we are. We have been waiting on God. We have strengthened our minds in the word. We know He is the Great I AM who can do anything. We have remembered what He has done in the past. We know He will take care of our future. He will not disappoint us. But sometimes our heart still cries out to God – How long Lord? Open my eyes to see, Lord!

A friend of mine who had been praying about a relationship with her estranged daughter, was greatly encouraged by the story of Abraham and Isaac. She related how God had showed her that even as Abraham was struggling with sacrificing his son, God had already sent a ram up the other side of the mountain. Abraham did not see the ram, until just the 'right moment' when God allowed him to see it. As my friend placed her daughter in God's hands, hope began to arise within her that God had sent a ram up the other side of the mountain and it would arrive at just the right time. She prayed that God would open her eyes to see what He was doing. Today she and her daughter are being restored.

...Show diligence
so as to realize the full assurance of HOPE.

Hebrews 6:11 (ASV)

There is an old illustration I heard many years ago. A man was in his cabin one day when God appeared to him. The Lord told him He had work for him to do. He then showed him a rock outside his cabin. The man was told to push against the stone with all his might. So the man did this – day after day. He toiled at pushing for many years, but nothing happened. The stone never moved. The man began to get discouraged and tired.

Since the man was discouraged, Satan decided to come into the scene and said – you've been pushing at that rock a long time, but nothing has happened. It hasn't even budged. Nothing has changed. Better give up. The man felt like a failure, but decided to take his problem to the Lord.

He said, "What's wrong? Why am I failing?"

The Lord responded to him in love, "My friend, when I gave you the task of pushing the stone – I never said you had to move it. Your task was only to push. Look at yourself and see how strong you have

become. You have done as I asked. Now, my friend
– I will move the rock for you.

At times when God speaks to us we try to figure
out how everything will work out. Just obey Him
– exercise faith and stand in hope. But know that it is
still God who moves the mountain!

- When everything seems to go wrong
  – P.U.S.H.
- When the job gets you down – P.U.S.H.
- When things don't turn out as you think they
  should – P.U.S.H.
- When your money is gone and bills are due
  – P.U.S.H.

There's an easy way to remember to P.U.S.H.

P = pray

U = until

S = something

H = happens

You can't go back for a new beginning, but you
can start now to make a new ending. Maybe some
of us are becoming stronger, more mature Christians
because of our pushing.

Show me your ways O Lord, teach me your path;,
guide me in your truth and teach me.
for You are God, my Savior,
and My HOPE is in You all day long.

Psalm 25:4,5 (NIV)

The name Elohim means – the Creator. It's a Hebrew word for God that appears in the first sentence of the Bible. In the beginning Elohim created the heaven and earth. It's used 2,570 times in the Bible.1

Genesis 1:26-28 says, so Elohim created mankind in His image, in the image of God He created them – male and female. Think about it – God is your creator. He formed you specifically, thoughtfully, carefully, individually, and precisely the way you are.

So then – if you have ever struggled with self-image, if you have ever cried over your family of origin, if you've ever resented your father and mother, if you've been unhappy with your physical limitation – or your reflection in the mirror........

Run to the Strong Tower again – the name of Elohim.

Colossians 1:16 says that all things were created BY Him and FOR Him. So we are created precisely the way we are – FOR HIM. Let's look at the Word and keep Elohim in mind. Psalm 139:13-15 says, 'Thou didst form my inward parts –Thou didst weave me in my mother's womb. I will give thanks to Thee for I am fearfully and wonderfully made. Wonderful are your works…..my frame was made in secret and skillfully wrought."

-created by Him-

Have you ever thought of yourself as fearfully and wonderfully made? Carefully and lovingly designed and made by a wise God. Your face may never be on a magazine. You may never be asked to model. You may never feel confident standing before a group. But I can tell you this – your conception, no matter the circumstances was no accident. God does not make mistakes! You are exactly as Elohim designed you to be.

Remember when Moses complained he wasn't eloquent but slow of speech and tongue in Exodus 14. What was God's reply to him? Who makes him dumb or deaf – seeing or blind? Is it not I the Lord?

This was always difficult for me to understand. It would leave questions in my mind. "You mean God made someone that way?" As we go on we will see the purpose here. In John 9, is the story of the man blind from birth. Jesus said that it was so that the works of God might be displayed in him. Now, I'm not a theologian or a philosopher – but – why would God create people who are different? Why would He permit what we would call a disability? I'm not sure we will have all the answers until we are on the 'other side' someday. But we need to take God's word for it.

Let's look at verse 2 here. The disciples asked the same question – who made him this way – was it because his parents sinned? What was Jesus answer to this – that Elohim might be displayed in him.

Again in Proverbs 18:10 – the name of the Lord is a strong tower – run to it!!! If you're not happy with yourself, your past, your limitations – run to Elohim. You may never have all the answers but you can display (glorify) God with your being.

You might not understand how your situation could ever bring Him glory. But He does not ask you to understand. He only asks you to trust in the name of the Lord. (Isaiah 50:10) Trust in the name of Elohim.

There are some wonderful words for us in Isaiah 43. Here it says that the Lord your Creator (Elohim) – He who formed you, I am the Lord. You are precious in my sight. Everyone who is called by My Name and whom I have created for my glory – whom I have formed, even whom I have made.

Elohim created you for His glory. Glory means to give a correct opinion or estimate of. So we are to live in such a way as to give a correct opinion or estimate of who God is. In Revelation 4, we read that He created all things and because of His will – they were created. You were created for His pleasure – His will.

So go before God and look at the course of your life. Are you fulfilling the purpose of your creation? What is keeping you from being or doing what you were created for? What do you need to change? To know Elohim —- is to know your reason for breathing.

Our Creator wants us to be grateful for the provisions we have right now and not try to control what we cannot control. Being grateful is so simple – but sometimes it's hard to do.

There was a study conducted in a restaurant. People were asked to sit at a table with a tablecloth that had one tiny black ink spot. The food and the service were fantastic. But when asked later to rate the restaurant – most people only commented on the stain. Their eyes were so focused on what wasn't right that they couldn't appreciate what was right.

Let's focus on what God has made for us. God open our eyes.

...that the eyes of your heart be enlightened,
in order that you may have HOPE....
the riches of His glorious inheritance...
and His great power for us who believe.

Ephesians 1:18-19 (NIV)

We read in II Kings 6 that Elisha's servant panicked when he saw the army of chariots and horses circling the city. What were they going to do? Elisha prayed, asking God to open His servant's eyes. The servant was astonished at what he saw. No matter who is against us God is for us. Ask God to open your eyes to the way He is working in your life. Then we learned in the story of Hagar in Genesis 21, how God opened her eyes to see the water He had provided for her and her son.

Now we come to I Kings 18. There was a severe famine and drought. The king sends Obadiah to look for water to keep the animals alive. But there is nothing – not even a sign of rain. Elijah says there is a 'sound' of rain. Ah, there's hope. The servant is told to go back and look again. He does this seven times. Then He sees a cloud as small as a man's hand. That's not much of a cloud to expect rain from – but it's hope again.

He then tells the king to go in his chariot before the heavy rain stops him. In a little while the sky grew black, (bigger hope) and then there was the heavy, long awaited rain.

Our prayer could be, Lord, give me a sign of hope to go with the promise you gave to me.

You are my hiding place and my shield....
I HOPE in your word.

Psalm 119:114 (NKJ)

-hope for dry bones-

In Ezekiel 37, God sat Ezekiel down in the middle of a valley of dry bones and then asked him a question, "Ezekiel, can these bones live?" Ezekiel was wise to answer that only God knew the answer to that.

God then tells Ezekiel to prophesy to these bones – "Hear the Word of the Lord". He continues to prophesy over the bones that God will cause breath to enter them that they may come to life.

110

This whole chapter is a great story of hope. I wonder how Ezekiel felt when he was placed in the valley of dry bones. But he did exactly as God told him to.

I believe that there are some reading these words today that God is asking the same question.

- Can these dead dreams live?
- Can this marriage live again?
- Can these children be saved?
- Can your body be healed?
- Can your finances be restored?

What do you say? Can they be?

-speak the Word-

In Ezekiel it said to speak the word of the Lord over the situation. His word brings light into the situation (Psalm 119:130) This promise is from God Himself, who makes the dry bones live again and speaks future events with as much certainty as though they were already past. (Romans 4:17)

We have all heard stories of people in a coma who are still aware of what is happening around them. Sometimes a patient later has confessed to feeling as if he were trapped in his body and unable to respond to his family. So speak as if they can hear. Speak life! How does faith come? By hearing what God thinks, what God says and what God can do.

So speak to those dead marriages. Speak to your children. Speak to your finances. Speak to your body.

Speak the word of the Lord. Speak in the spirit realm and tell it to come in line with the word of the Lord and with the plan of God.

Ezekiel 12 says that we have eyes to see but do not see and ears to hear but do not hear.

-spiritual eyes-

I want you to give your eyes to the Lord. Tell Him you want to see what He sees. Tell Him you want to see what He is doing. Ask for your eyes to be opened so that you might see Him instead of focusing on the things of this world.

Show me a sign for good....because You, O Lord, have helped me and comforted me.

Psalm 86:17

In the morning I will order my prayer to You and eagerly wait.

Psalm 5:3

They said, "Lord we want our eyes to be opened".

Matthew 20:33

....may our Lord Jesus Christ Himself and God
our Father, who loved us
and by His grace gave us eternal encouragement
and HOPE, encourage your hearts.

II Thessalonians 2:16-17 (NIV)

Questions for discussion and reflection

1. What does" prophesy over these bones" mean to you?

2. What is the purpose God created you for?

3. Read Psalm 130 and give a word of testimony.

Hope Scriptures

Chapter 1

Hebrews 6:17-18
(NIV)

God wanted to make the unchanging nature of His purpose very clear to the heirs of what was promised, He confirmed it with an oath. God did this so that, by two unchangeable things in which it is impossible for God to lie, we who have fled to take hold of the HOPE offered to us may be greatly encouraged.

Romans 15:4
(ASV)

For whatever was written in earlier times – was written for our instruction, that through perseverance and the encour-agement of the scriptures we might have HOPE.

Romans 4:18 (NKJ)	Abraham – who contrary to hope in HOPE believed, … according to what was spoken.
Romans 15:13 (NKJ)	May the God of HOPE fill you with all joy and peace in believing, that you may abound in HOPE by the power of the Holy Spirit.

Chapter 2

Hebrews 6:19 (NIV)	We have this HOPE as an anchor for the soul, firm and secure.
Psalm 42:5,11 (NIV)	Why are you downcast, O my soul? Why so disturbed within me? Put your HOPE in God, For I will yet praise Him, my Savior and my God.
Psalm 33:18 (NIV)	The eyes of the Lord are on those who fear Him, on those whose HOPE is in His unfailing love.

Chapter 3

Psalm 130:5 (NIV)	I wait for the Lord, my soul wait, and in His Word do I HOPE.

Hebrews 10:23 (NIV)	Let us hold unswervingly to the HOPE we profess, for He who promised is faithful.
Psalm 62:5 (NIV)	Find rest, O my soul, in God alone; my HOPE comes from Him. He alone is My rock and my salvation; He is my fortress, I will not be shaken.
Psalm 119:81 (NIV)	My soul faints with longing.... but I have put my HOPE in your word.

Chapter 4

I Thessalonians 5:8 (ASV)	Put on the breastplate of faith and love,... and as a helmet the Hope of salvation (deliverance).
Romans 8:25 (NKJ)	If we HOPE for what we do not see, we eagerly wait for it with perseverance.
I Peter 1:13 (ASV)	Gird your minds for action... fix your HOPE completely on the grace brought to you at the revelation of Jesus Christ.

Chapter 5

Psalm 78:7 (NKJ)	Set your HOPE in God (confidence) and do not forget the works of God.
Psalm 146:5 (NIV)	Blessed is he whose help is the God of Jacob, whose HOPE is in the Lord his God.
Jeremiah 17:7 (NKJ)	Blessed is the man who trusts in the Lord, whose HOPE is in the Lord.

Chapter 6

Lamentations 3:19-23 (NIV) I remember my affliction and my wandering, the bitterness and The gall... my soul is downcast within me. Yet this I call to mind and therefore I have HOPE: because of the Lord's great love we are not consumed, for His compassions never fail. They are new every morning; Great is your faithfulness.

Jeremiah 29:11 - (ASV) For I know the plans that I have for you, declares the Lord, plans for welfare and not for calamity to give you a future and a HOPE.

| Psalm 119:49 (NIV) | Remember your word to your servant, for You have given me HOPE. |

Chapter 7

| Proverbs 13:12 (ASV) | HOPE deferred makes the heart sick, but a desire fulfilled is a tree of life. |

| Psalm 38:15 (ASV) | For I HOPE in Thee, O Lord, Thou wilt answer, O Lord my God. |

| Ezra 10:2 (NKJ) | ....there is HOPE in Israel in spite of this. |

| Jeremiah 31:17 (NIV) | There is HOPE for your future, declares the Lord, your children shall return to their own land. |

Chapter 8

| Romans 5:5 (NKJ) | HOPE does not disappoint, because the love of God has been poured out in our hearts by the Holy Spirit who was given to us. |

Zechariah 9:12
(ASV)

Return to the stronghold, O prisoners, who have the HOPE, this very day I am declaring that I will restore double to you.

Colossians 1:23
(ASV)

Continue in the faith firmly established and steadfast, notmoved away from the HOPE...

II Corinthians 1:10
(ASV)

Set our HOPE on He who will yet deliver us.

Chapter 9

Hebrews 6:11
(ASV)

...Show diligence so as to realize the full assurance of HOPE. until the end.

Psalm 25:4,5
(NIV)

Show me your ways, O Lord, teach me your path; guide me in your truth and teach me, for You are God, my Savior, and my HOPE is in You all day long.

Ephesians 1:18,19
(NIV)

...that the eyes of your heart may be enlightened in order that you may know the HOPE ... the riches of His glorious inheritance... and His great power for us who believe.

Psalm 119:114
(NKJ)

You are my hiding place and my shield... I HOPE in your word.

II Thessalonians 2:16,17
(NIV)

May our Lord Jesus Christ Himself andGod our Father, who loved us and by His grace gave us eternal encouragement and good HOPE, encourage your hearts....

Notes

Chapter One – Hope Again

1. Nicole Johnson, *Irrepressible Hope,* (W Publishing Group/Nelson 2003) 42.

2. Alton Garrison, *Pentecostal Evangel,* (July 29, 2007) 22.

Chapter Two – Hope - God Sees

1. Nicole Johnson, *Irrepressible Hope,* (W Publishing Group/Nelson 2003) 41.

2. Ann Spangler, *Praying the Names of God,* (Zondervan 2004) 27.

Chapter Three – Hope - Waiting on God

1. Kay Arthur, *The Peace and Power of Knowing God's Name,* (Waterbrook Press/ Random House, Inc. 2002) 42.

Chapter Four – Hope- Gird your Mind

1. Joyce Meyer, *I Dare You,*

Chapter Five - Hope – the Great I AM

1. Nicole Johnson, *Irrepressible Hope,* (W Publishing Group/Nelson 2003) 183.

Chapter Six – Hope – Remembrances

1. Ann Spangler, *Praying the Names of God,* (Zondervan 2004) 171.

Chapter Seven-Hope – for your future

1. Tracy Dartt, *God on the Mountain*, Gaviota Music, % Manna Music, 1975

Chapter Eight – Hope – does not disappoint

1. Nicole Johnson, *Irrepressible Hope*, (W Publishing Group/Nelson 2003) 232

2. Ann Spangler, *Praying the Names of God*, (Zondervan 2004) 182

Chapter Nine – Hope-open my eyes

1. Ann Spangler, *Praying the Names of God*, (Zondervan 2004) 15

Printed in the United States
207338BV00001B/235-600/P

9 781606 476871